Thinking about Mac and Tab

Primary Phonics COMPREHENSION

WORKBOOK 3

Educators Publishing Service, Inc.

Cambridge and Toronto

Thinking about Mac and Tab: Primary Phonics Comprehension

Text by Karen L. Smith

Illustrations by Anslie G. Philpot

Design by Persis Barron Levy

....

Educators Publishing Service, Inc.

ISBN 0-8388-2383-1
Printed in U.S.A.

Contents

Match.

The sled did stop.

Skip got his skates.

"I can slide and spin."

Circle yes or no.

Did Skip skate on the steep slope?

Yes   **No**

Fill in the puzzle with words from the story.

Across

1. "Let me slide

   on the _____,"

   said Skip.

   (page 2)

Down

1. "I can skate,"

   said _____.

   (page 9)

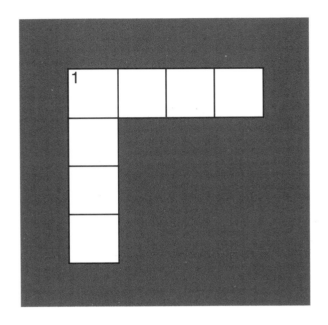

Draw or write.

What did Skip ride on the slope?

Match.

The tune made her smile.

"I will sleep here."

Luz had meat and beans.

Circle yes or no.

Can the plane take off in the fog?

Yes   No

Fill in the puzzle with words from the story.

Across

1. Luz sat in her _____. (page 3)

Down

2. "Plug it in and hear a _____." (page 10)

Draw or write.

Where did Luz go on the plane?

Match.

"Put him in," said Fran.

Spot did scare the cat.

Cleve and Fran got cones.

Circle yes or no.

Was Cleve the name of the dog?

Yes   **No**

Fill in the puzzle with words from the story.

Across

1. "A dog can not sleep
   in the _____."
   (page 9)

Down

2. "I need to get Spot up
   and _____ him
   home," said Cleve.
   (page 5)

Draw or write.

What woke Spot up?

Match.

"We can roast hot dogs."

"His swim fins made the prints."

"I did not see a beast."

. . . .

Circle yes or no.

Did Steve and Greg set up the tent in the stream?

Yes   **No**

Fill in the puzzle with words from the story.

Across

1. Steve and Greg came to a _____. (page 1)

Down

2. "We can _____ hot dogs." (page 5)

Draw or write.

How did the big prints get on the sand?

Match.

"Time to go to sleep."

"Jump up," said the elf.

The ant is so big.

Circle yes or no.

Did Glen get lost in Elf Land in his dream?

Yes   **No**

10

Fill in the puzzle with words from the story.

Across

1. "I am big,"
   said _____.
   (page 5)

Down

2. "I am lost in
   Elf _____,"
   said Glen.
   (page 11)

Draw or write.

How did Glen get home from Elf Land?

Write numbers under each box to put them in the correct order.

_____

_____

_____

Cleve went home and made a gift.

_____

Circle yes or no.

Did Cleve get a plant at the store?

Yes   No

Draw or write.

What did Cleve spend his last dime on?

Circle the correct word to fill in the blank.

The _____ went in the drain in the street.

dimes   domes

Draw.

Cleve had just a dime. How did he feel on page 9?

Write numbers under each box to put them in the correct order.

_____

The fireman gave the kitten to Sue.

_____

....

Circle yes or no.

Did the kitten sleep in his basket?

Yes   No

Draw or write.

What did Sue put in the basket to make it a soft bed?

Circle the correct word to fill in the blank.

"Take the _____ inside," said Dad. "It is bedtime."

kitten   kite

Draw.

How did Mittens like the top of the pole?

Write numbers under each box to put them in the correct order.

_____

_____

"I am so glad the seagulls are well," said Bill.

_____

_____

Circle yes or no.

Did Bill toss bits of hot dog up in the air?

Yes   **No**

Draw or write.

How can a sea gull rest one leg?

Circle the correct word to fill in the blank.

"Please pass me a _____ and I will fill it up with limeade."

grass   glass

Draw.

How did Bill feel on page 5?

Write numbers under each box to put them in the correct order.

"Wait," said the duck. "I am not mean. I am lost."

_____

_____

The duck swam to his flock.

_____

_____

· ·

Circle yes or no.

Did the cricket kick the egg?

Yes   No

Draw or write.

What was inside the egg?

....

Circle the correct word to fill in the blank.

"Go to the pond and jump in," said the _____.

flock   rabbit

....

Draw.

How did the duck feel on page 9?

Write numbers under each box to put them in the correct order.

_____

Max went to the mailbox to get the mail.

_____

"Jill likes the fox," said Max. "And I like the real cake."

_____

Circle yes or no.

Did Jill and Max eat the cakes made of sand?

Yes   No